AF454350

KIDS LIFE

JOHAN MARTIN

KIDS LIFE
Johan Martin

ILLUSTRATIONS
Lubomír Lichý

2ND EDITION

HANZESTAD PUBLICATIONS

ISBN
978 907 0506 193

NUR
370 – 450 – 840 – 854 – 773

HAPPY QUOTES

TABLE OF CONTENTS

The Beginning is the most Important Part of the Work.

Plato

Greek Philosopher – Athene

427 BC – 347 BC

A BABY IS COMING

But a new car doesn't say, daddy!

Does daddy know?

ung......diddla...bow......WOW.
uchy

BODY DISCOVERY

Whooooahh

Mommy............done.

Help!! The mute button.

Can't help it.
At night my eyes are closed.

Hurry up......me potty too!

She's in her underpants!

Mommy says
Baking me was a success.

I have a mild concussion?
Then he has a heavy concussion!

That woman has big ones!!

And you haven't read lesson 7 yet grandma!

Only where Children Gather is there any real Chance of Fun.

Mignon McLaughlin,
Journalist Florida USA
1913 – 1983

MOMMY

No assholes today mom?

Mommy!

Is that so you won't go bad?

He doesn't eat vegetables either.

You're acting like a five-year old.
I am five!

Unless you can explain it to your grandmother, you don't Really Understand something.

Albert Einstein

Nobel Prize: Physics GERMANY – USA

1879 – 1955

GRANDMA

I have to go grandma.

I already have 1 birthday guestses.

Your mouth is not as big
as daddy said.

Pocket money?? I have no pocket.

The kids look after grandma.

I'll take him to the beach Mom.

KIDS LEARN FAST

Daddy and I were in London.

They all speak with an accent there.

Very funny!

An only child?

What luck to your parents!

Jimmy wants to become a firefighter and
Nancy wants to become old.....and.....?

I watched the barber do it.

From the moment I could talk,
I wanted to be a racing driver!

Can you do it without moving your left arm?

MUSIC

His girlfriend is an Elvis fan!

How many keys are there
per measure?

A dollar from mommy to practice.
A dollar from dad to quit for a while!

We play songs........ from the time
they were still in!

In the end you have to Love.
Finally you have to Start Loving
in order not to Get Sick
and you have to fall ill
if you Cannot Love as a result
of Failure.

Sigmund Freud

Psychiatrist Vienna, Austria

1856–1939

LOVE

Not in his creative phase yet I see!

I won't pull your finger again.
Your farts stink!

You're no fun!
I'm gonna erase you.

What did my strong Michael say
daddy should wait for?
Till I'm as tall as you are!

Bobby

You learn more from your Children than they do from you They learn a world from you that is no more. You learn one from them, which is now becoming valid.

Friedrich Rückert 1788 –1866)

German poet, translator

professor of Oriental languages.

PHILOSOPHY

Mommy, can you choose that yourself?

Yes, I think I'm in love now.

Mommy says: kids are bad for your
carrrrrrreer!

It doesn't work that way, Dad.

I won't take up sports
It looks more fun than it really is!

If you are rich you already have everything... and...
you have everything...you don't need any more money!

Tall grown people can't play anymore.
They look after the kids.

Birds die more beautifully
than Dinos.

You are the giraffe and I am the owl.
I'm more of a night person.

In ten years I will be too old for a dress.

Pretend we're sleeping, then he will stop.

THE END

*A child can teach an adult
three things:
To be happy for no reason.
To always be busy with something,
and to know how to demand
with all his might that,
which he desires.*

Paulo Coelho de Souza Born 1947

Brazilian lyricist and novelist

Notable works: The Alchemist

Send and win

YOUR KID SAYS FUNNY THINGS

WIN A POSTER

SEND A QUOTE

I WILL MAKE THE DRAWING

Send and win

WWW.JOHANMARTINCARTOONS.COM

I thank all readers who contributed to this edition
by sending children's quotes.

Johan Martin

BOOKS/EPUBS
At your bookshop

POSTERS
www.etsy.com/shop/JOHANMARTINCARTOONS

MORE CARTOONS
WWW.JOHANMARTINCARTOONS.COM

INFO
INFO@JOHANMARTINCARTOONS.COM
We will be pleased to answer your questions